SUCCESS PRINCIPLES POST COVID-19

Guiding Principles to Chart Your Path to Success

GAVIN DUBUISSON

SUCCESS PRINCIPLES, POST COVID-19

Guiding Principles to Chart Your Path to Success

©2020 GAVIN DUBUISSON

print ISBN: 978-1-09832-992-1

ebook ISBN: 978-1-09832-993-8

CONTENTS

FORWARD

There are hundreds of books written on the subject of success. Most all center around "methods" to attain your desires such as money, and promise a success filled life.

The difference presented here is nine "principles" of success. A principle is a law or fact of nature that explains the how or why something happens.

Anyone experienced with flying understands the importance of having a detailed flight plan before starting a flight to assure success in reaching your destination. The business world also requires you to prepare equally for your career path to success. Any plan must allow for adjustments along the way BUT the core "principles" remain the same.

The core principles presented in this book are the same weather you have been in business one year or ten years. Failure in business is often the result of short sighted thinking coupled with a belief that once you have reached a certain level of success, all will automatically continue. It WILL NOT unless your SUCCESS MENTALITY is focused on all nine of the principles presented for lifetime SUCCESS.

Success is NOT simple! Success is NOT easy! It is NOT about money, status, owning things, or lifestyle. IT IS PEACE OF MIND, JOY, SENSE OF SELF WORTH, PURPOSE IN LIFE ATTAINED, PERSONAL GRATITUDE, AND LOVE FOR OTHERS!

CHARACTER

Character is a principle that reflects who you are as a human being. It is your core beliefs such as integrity, ethics, morals, truthfulness, probity and others.

Although I support some of the current thoughts like visualization, affirmations and positive thinking, character has to be developed and practiced as a conscious personal belief principal to attain lasting Success. You can't buy it or fake it till you make it!

All nine principles presented here are important for personal and professional success. However I believe character is the foundation for the other eight.

We do not have to look far in today's world to find many examples of others who claim character as a virtue although in reality we discover they are counterfeit in their actions. For example, make your choice in any area of life during the recent past such as marriage, politics, self centeredness, abuse, religion, business, sports, professional relationships, etc. and you will see examples of many lives and millions of dollars thrown away by betrayal of one's character. In fact our prison system is full of examples. We hear about these every day and wonder what would cause someone to dishonor their character and betray many people after reaching a level of success that others aspire to. The real test is does your belief system measure up to your self image and as others see you?

In today's world Character often is not visible until you make poor choices at which time others are surprised that a individual sabotaged themselves. For example, the game of golf is perhaps the only game where the participant must keep their on scores and call penalties on themselves requiring a high level of character. But we have witnessed some of the worlds greatest professional golfers destroy their career and marriage by making poor choices in life. Your character is exposed in all areas of your life and requires your attention as principle number one if you hope to achieve lasting Success.

We all have moments where our true character is put to the test. Our success will be defined as we individually respond to those test. Constant attention to ourself is required no matter what status we attain in life.

ACTION PROJECT: CHARACTER

Therefore your first assignment in your personal pursuit of success is the following. After researching "CharacterTraits", make a list of your current character traits in your life as reflected to others. Next, rate yourself honestly as you really are in each area 1-10 (10 being highest). Then list other traits that you would like to incorporate in your life as you develop this new model for success.

Obliviously none of us are perfect but awareness of strengths and weakness can promote improvement. If we loose desire to grow personally and professionally, our death has already started.

"TO THY OWN SELF BE TRUE"

Shakespeare

CLARITY

Clarity represents understanding of ourself as we go through life. Clarity is also very important as we build relationships with others especially in our efforts to create trust through transparency.

If we begin with character, it is easier to develop clarity. Therefore you can see why the building blocks of our character traits are critical as we seek clarity for our own lives in pursuit of success.

Clarity is not as simple as it sounds. In the business world we are often held to corporate standards developed in your job description (the corporate world loves to tell you how to think). However we must also maintain clarity in our personal lives to fulfill our individual requirements as well.

The skill of goal setting is usually touted as necessary for success but without clarity goal setting is only a exercise usually built around your companies model of expectations rather than yours. It may be fulfilling to meet company goals but what about your own goals in your personal success model?

You must have clarity in goal setting techniques as it relates to your personal success model. The good news is that clarity can be a learned skill. The greater challenge will be remaining true to your company while not loosing sight of you personal model.

This makes your character traits even more important as you strive to remain true to your company and self at the same time. It also explains why so many people are miserable in their career. The ideal solution is have your own business that matches your character traits.

We frequently see examples of those who are not fulfilled in their career choice. They are often trying to develop clarity in a environment that does not match up to their expectations. If you find yourself telling others that you are just trying to get by or that you hate your job or you wish you could start life over, then you are not likely to have clarity in either your business or personal life.

The ability to set priorities (goals) is the result of clarity. Therefore you can see the challenge of finding happiness in a corporate environment that exist for the benefit of stockholders. There are those who accomplish clarity in the corporate world because it helps them develop clarity in their personal life providing fulfillment in both areas.

If you are blessed to have your own business, the process of developing clarity is a easier task. Either way your self identity is critical to achieve true success even if you must remain in a corporate world.

If you must exist in a dual world of the Corporate and your own personal world it is critical to adopt my concept of PRIDE (Performance Requires Individual Dedicated Effort). PRIDE connects a character trait in each world that assist you in development of clarity for both.)

ACTION PROJECT : CLARITY

Your reviews with your company should provide you with a idea where you stand with them. They provide the guidance and supervision to assist you.

However your objective here is to apply these principles to your personal success. If you have your own business, recognize that you are blessed. Revisit the character traits you process and begin to develop clarity in your business plan including priorities

in all areas.

Review your plan regularly and utilize

PRIDE to complete objectives.

COMMITMENT

Commitment is a critically important principle in our pursuit of success in both the personal and professional areas of life. Our commitment is only meaningful once we understand our character traits and then have clarity in our life. Otherwise we are simply committed on a trial and error basis for short periods in life depending on the stage we are in at the moment.

The problem is during life most people go through many changing stages. We learn at a very young age that we must remain committed to the moment since we rarely have studied the principles in this book as a whole. Then we encounter a constantly changing environment and must begin a new cycle. Many become discouraged and end up confused for most of life regarding their MAIN COMMITMENT PRINCIPLE of SUCCESS.

Additionally there are many situations in life that will require commitment for a time. For example, pursuit of a education, a relationship, a fitness program, our children, family, etc. However if overall success is to be attained, we must establish our overall purpose personally and never loose sight of the real commitment requiring focus on a constant basis even as we deal with many other short range commitments.

Remember our definition of success as presented in the forward of this book - "peace of mind, joy, sense of self worth, purpose in life attained, personal gratitude and love for others".

If this sounds confusing it is because I'm referring to a concept that some spend a lifetime trying to determine. It is called your PASSION! You either live life SEEKING your passion or LIVING your passion. I conduct a workshop on helping others determine their passion. We are blessed in deed once we realize our passion.

We may be blessed with a wonderful marriage, loving children, grandchildren or a great career. However all this will change over time. This is why people often die after loosing a lifetime spouse or after retiring from a lifetime career. They have lost their passion. It is sad to watch those who have had all the above only to reach a point in life where they can't stand being alone.

My passion has not become clear until late in life. For me, it is giving myself to help others continue to grow in their personal and professional life thus attaining success as defined above.

Our greatest gift from God is the power of choice. Our commitment to all those in our life is most fulfilling with a passion for life with purpose for ourself, those we love and others.

There is a big difference in involvement and commitment that is illustrated in the bacon and eggs breakfast. The chicken is involved but the pig is committed! Know the difference in your life.

ACTION PROJECT: COMMITMENT

Spend meditation time each day on your commitments like family, career and other areas of gratitude in you life. Are you CLEAR on your PASSION? Are you driven by your PASSION in any areas? If not, then why? The commitment to YOUR PASSION is the central theme of your success.

Contact me for my passion workshop dates and to be on my mailing list as I release my new book soon.

"DISCOVERING YOUR PASSION"

CREATIVITY

Most of us have a definition of creativity in mind when asked. However creativity is critical when referred to as one of the nine principals of success discussed here. One of the biggest obstacles throughout life is the ability to adjust to ever changing circumstances that life throws our way. This biggest obstacle I am speaking of is CHANGE!

It is this kind of change that I refer to as the many different kinds of DRAMA we see in others throughout life. I call it OPD (other peoples drama!). If you have a loving and caring tendency, you will naturally desire to help others in their struggle with life's many forms of drama. Although it may be well intended on your part it can soon become "your" drama instead of OPD. I have had to remind myself frequently through many years of managing and coaching others that "your drama is not my mama"! It's not your responsibility to FIX others. The most you can hope for is helping them learn these principles of success in order to pursue the definition of success we have established. It may sound selfish but remember the greatest power we ALL equally possess is the power of choice. Heal thy self so that others will utilize the principles of success as defined in our Forward.

So creativity discussed here deals with the ability to handle changes in life in a creative way. Helping yourself and others who seek SUCCESS learn to focus on these nine principles will create a attitude of problem solving rather than constant focus on OPD.

One of my daughters shared her recent awareness in dealing with personal relationships. Her conclusion was to pull away from OPD if it did not serve her personally. She is one of the most caring and loving people I know with much to give to others but I see the maturing approach she is committed to in her success walk through life.

Here is a example of the creative approach utilizing focus on solutions rather than problems as you seek success on life: The FBI was interviewing to recruit a new agent and wanted to test the applicants ability to be creative with problems they might encounter in their work. They brought in the first guy and gave him a loaded gun with instructions to enter a secret room where his spouse waited and eliminate her. He entered but soon returned to explain he could not do it and was no longer interested in the position. A second guy was brought in and given the gun with the same instructions. He also returned shortly expressing regret he could not do it and was no longer interested. The third applicant was a woman. They presented the gun along with instructions. She entered the room firing the gun six times. Then a loud noise including fighting and screaming occurred. Finally the wife stumbled out of the room complaining that the gun seemed to contain blanks but she was successful in beating him to death with a chair! Now that's commitment, clarity and creativity!!!

Women seem to have a more free spirited approach to being creative in dealing with emotions. Men tend to be more pragmatic in dealing with problems that exist in specific situations. Learn to " think OUTSIDE the box" when faced with change.

ACTION PROJECT: CREATIVITY

How creative are you in all areas of your life. Conduct a brain storming session with yourself. List all areas making note of how you might be more creative in your current situation when confronted with inevitable change!

How did you respond to the Covid-19 Pandemic? Did you grow through the total change required by all or did you surrender to the old normal instead of invitation for a new normal?

CREDITABILITY

Creditability deserves your attention as you learn the nine important areas of your success building blocks. This is a often overlooked principle as we climb the success latter. Let me illustrate why this is so important.

A number of years back I was faced with a cancer diagnosis. Now THAT is life or death CHANGE! After I dealt with the initial shock I remembered one of my core beliefs about problems which is that all problems only come in two forms. Those we can NOT change and those we CAN! I realized I could not change the diagnosis of cancer (a problem) so I accepted the problem. However I did have a "choice"in how to deal with the (situation) which I could change. Therefore I changed my focus to the situation and began the learning curve regarding my particular cancer and the possibility of remission.

The medical world is making incredible progress with all cancers and I believe it will be a thing of the past in the not to distant future. Mine happened to be a type that ranked number two in deaths for men. After research I reached a decision on the kind of Doctor I would seek out.

This is where CREDITABILITY became my focus. I could choose a Dr that had numerous years in dealing with my type of cancer OR I could choose a young Dr with proven credentials who was up to speed with the latest methods of treatment. While the older Dr had more experience, I did not want someone who had reached a point in life who was resistant to CHANGE. I knew from experience that some professionals reach a point in life where they are more concerned about their golf score or cocktail hour after a long day than continued growth in their profession. As a result I choose a young Dr with passion and numerous successful results in the type surgery treatment I elected. Although there are no guarantees in life, we do have choice in who we do business with. I have been blessed and have not had any further cancer for eighteen years.

The intent of sharing my own story is to encourage young professionals to not fear the older client since the older person often prefers a younger professional provided they have credibility and a passion to help others. Older folks automatically assume the older professional has CREDITABILITY because of age. However, there is more to CREDITABILITY than age alone.

ACTION PROJECT: CREDITABILITY

This fourth principle of success, requires you to always be mindful of your continued professional development no matter your age or experience. A large client base will validate your CREDITABILITY as time passes. In the mean time you must continue to grow professionally and personally.

CFO ATTITUDE

The CFO ATTITUDE is your basis for development of this sixth very important SUCCESS principle! My CFO stands for

CUSTOMER FIRST ORIENTATION and is critical for your implementation in your own business. If your career is with a large corporation, this may be a huge challenge since I find more companies give lip service to customer service rather than follow through.

My first job after college was with Sears in a management training program. Looking back now I realize it was some of the best training I would ever receive in my life. Sears had a standing customer policy for everyone of "satisfaction guaranteed or your money back". That visible sign was on all the entrance doors and throughout the store.

The second largest department in the store was the catalogue shopping section. I was assigned to the catalogue department as a assistant manager with instructions to always remember that my first responsibility was to satisfy the customer or provide their money back. Everything Sears sold was in the catalog department where we had six sales associates and a phone bank of twenty five sales associates. Beside learning how to manage others, I learned how to negotiate with unhappy customers. For example, If a customer had used a lawn mower for six months and then decided they wanted a full refund, I would have to reason with them that certainly they had received some benefit and therefore should be satisfied with a partial refund.

My communication and negotiating skills were developed at a very young age as a result. A more critical lesson I learned was the importance of having a mentor. I still remember his name today (Mr Frank Lee). His people skills and ability to motivate a young kid is still appreciated today even though I'm sure he is long passed.

One thing that is very important in business is giving the customer a feeling of importance. Business seems to have developed a attitude over the past years of profit first and customer second. A emphasis on service, reliability, and quality is still a goal of everyone as their business is developed. This certainly provides a level of SUCCESS for yourself and the customer.

NOTE: Sears was a number one retailer many years. Employees shared in one of the best profit sharing plans in the retail industry. However, change caught up with the giant as many other big box stores were born. The big factor was the internet as a distribution marketing method. Even though Sears was clearly number one in the old fashion method of telephone marketing, they have had to close many stores because they failed to respond to the technology challenge. (CHANGE)!

They may be making a comeback now since they recently formed a partnership with the most successful retail business in the world - AMAZON!

The principle of CREATIVITY is thus illustrated as you must learn to constantly reinvent your SUCCESS. The CEO OF AMAZON HAS RECENTLY DISTINGUISHED HIMSELF AS THE WEALTHIEST PERSON IN THE WORLD REPLACING BILL GATES!

ACTION PLAN: FOR CFO ATTITUDE

Prospects, and customers alike want to know that we have a caring attitude about their problems. In other words they don't care how much we know until they know how much we care. Consider your clients and the people you serve. Remember to develop their loyalty. They must believe you are genuine and then you must show it. Give thought on how you can communicate that concept in your daily business. Soon you will experience your success because they will refer others to you regularly.

COMMUNICATION

My seventh SUCCESS principle of communication is more important today than ever. The key is to understand that communication with your customer is only ONE FACTOR! COMMUNICATION with your employees is even more critical to build lasting loyalty and commitment from the people that are responsible for those that make it happen for your business every day.

I am amazed that business today is so consumed with pleasing the Board of Directors and stockholders that they miss the group most responsible for their success. (The employee) A common mistake I see in doing staff workshops is their impression that they are not valued. I find myself trying to illustrate to the company that if they pay peanuts they will end up with monkeys. My success model of PEOPLEOLOGY (Building and Keeping Relationships) is more important to employees than to customers. Without employee buy in to management and commitment of employees there are NO CUSTOMERS.

Often what is needed is commitment to staff using a high touch approach rather than a mandate to "just get it done"! No wonder that recent college graduates will have a average of six to nine careers over their lifetime. That is the reason I often hear employees say they are just trying to get by until a better deal comes along. They learn early that profit is more important than people. They are then likely to pass that impression on to the customers as well.

Many managers do not understand why they fail at recruiting and developing loyal staff. But their staff will often tell me in confidence that they are MICRO MANAGED by someone who only cares about keeping their own job. I even had one manager tell me that it is easier to replace employees than to build loyalty and commitment.

Managements lack of understanding PEOPLEOLOGY will frequently transfer their attitudes to the customer. One manager who had survived many years let me know that the customer didn't matter since the customer didn't have many other choices.

The word I most often hear is "TEAM". It's generally conveyed by someone who has NO idea of what a team is and never been part of a team themselves since their company promotes great slogans like "people first" and then expects management to implement the principles without any training.

Remember as you begin to implement specific skills in each of my nine principles to consider yourself the company, the employee and the consumer. The foundation for yourself is the principles. However, to implement them is use of the skills. Never stop growing personally or professionally. There are many sources for continued development of communication skills.

ACTION PROJECT: COMMUNICATION

Devote study time specifically to better Communication skills. Remember, it takes effort. We see more evidence today than ever that true communication

Is not tweets or brief text. They serve a important role especially for quick personal communication. However, others important for your success will respond more to the personal feeling ofInteraction.

Remember our definition of SUCCESS established in the FORWARD:

IT IS PEACE OF MIND, JOY, SENSE OF SELF WORTH, PURPOSE IN LIFE ATTAINED, PERSONAL GRATITUDE, AND LOVE FOR OTHERS!

CONCEPTS

One of my main ideas in presenting these nine principles of SUCCESS is to challenge the traditional concepts that are generally associated with the definition of what success means. The traits you are becoming familiar with extend beyond things we normally think of when defining our success.

We often develop a strategy to accomplish our goals such as money, status, a big home, lavish lifestyle or things that can be seen to validate our accomplishments. However all of that can be lost or destroyed in a moment.

There is nothing wrong with desiring the things mentioned above but as you accomplish those goals it is usually never enough. There are many examples in life of those who acquired all the outward signs of success only to die miserable after realizing enough was

NEVER enough. It is often those with the most money, the fastest cars, etc. that end up with the broken lives, marriages, families, and unfulfilled purpose.

I had the opportunity to witness many people who realized late in life that their concept of success had been built on the wrong cornerstone.

Peace of mind, joy, sense of self worth, purpose in life attained, personal gratitude and love of others brings new concepts of success to light. It does not exclude the outward signs we typically associate with success but it does bring purpose and a more fulfilling journey.

My personal passion of helping others grow personally and professionally provides meaning for a well rounded life. I've noticed that the millinnials of today are generally not in a hurry for the outward signs of traditional success. Perhaps they have been witness to the many failures of those seeking happiness through "things".

Accept that success is multi faceted. There is nothing wrong with desiring the outward signs of wealth and status. However, consider the success concepts portrayed here with these nine principles as your foundation.

CONCEPTS: ACTION PLAN

My first published book was "101 Things I Want My Grandkids To Know Before I Go"(Business and Life Principles). It will soon be available as a ebook. One of my principles that I share is about time.

There are only two kinds of time. They are thinking time and doing time. My action plan for you is to utilize some of your thinking time each day to think about your traditional definition of success versus the nine principles learned and discussed here.

You must use these in your daily life or you will loose them. Began to study and commit to memory the characteristic of each.

CHALLENGED

Challenged is the ninth principle of success. You will never find success in business or life unless you are challenged. I have heard young people say they would do anything if the money was right. But they don't understand how miserable life can be if you don't enjoy getting out of bed every day and looking forward to your day. (PASION)

You will meet many people who quickly confess their unhappiness in where and what they spend the majority of their waking hours doing. That is NOT success as defined in our nine principles. That's hell on earth. If you don't learn anything else from this book, PLEASE remember that if you don't like what you're doing for a living, get the hell out and do something else! We can't erase bad decisions but we can stop and reboot our life. Some people worry more about how they look more than how they feel. A depressed, unhappy, tired unfulfilled life will kill you quicker than any disease and it is contagious to those around you.

The only difference in a rut and a grave is that the grave is closed at both ends. We have one of the most medicated, addicted, nations on earth and yet people will continue to live in fear of change.

If you don't feel challenged you will never reach your potential personally or professionally. Yes, life is not perfect and there will be times where you have to gut it out as you continue to survive. But remember adversity makes you bitter or better. Take a look around you if you want to see real suffering that some folks have to endure.

I have a personal aversion and disgust with the thumb suckers of the world. I also have more than my share of empathy and sympathy for those who really suffer with no options. I will support others till the end but remember mine is a tough love approach. Your drama is not my mama.

My final "challenge" is to learn GRIT. GRIT is mental toughness and courage in the face of hardship or danger.

CHALLENGED: ACTION PLAN

Your action plan for this ninth and last principle is important in order to benefit from the time you have invested so far.

Remember the difference in involvement and commitment? Commit to a study of the nine principles until they become a part of your own philosophy regarding SUCCESS. Study each one for a entire month doing a review at the end of the month of all nine.

As you develop other important skills like planning, goal setting, establishing priorities, etc., keep in mind that all the skills in the world will not last unless you have a lasting understanding of what SUCCESS really means.

PEOPLEOLOGY BONUS

PEOPLEOLOGY IS MY TERM FOR BUILDING AND KEEPING RELATIONSHIPS.

I'm including 20 FREE example concepts for your review. These relationship builders can be used to make your success journey easier and quicker.

1. Others would rather know how much you care before they care how much know

2. People will usually forget things you say or do but they never forget how you make them feel

3. Begin your relationship with others by asking questions about them (listen) before talking about yourself.

4. Avoid others whose life constantly revolves around drama. Don't let their drama become your MOMA!

5. If you manage others, remember to be fair does not mean to threat everyone equal and if you try to treat everyone equal does NOT mean you are being fair.

6. Learn the difference in empathy for others versus sympathy for others.

7. There is a difference in professional maturity and emotional maturity. Learn!

8. Learn the difference in a excuse and a REASON.

9. LEARN the difference in a situation and a FACT OF LIFE.

10. BUILD relationships with others who focus on the future more than the past.

11. Avoid others who spend time "thumb sucking" and "whining" about life or business.

12. Technology skills are important but PROPLEOLOGY skills build relationships and are number one for results.

13. Your ATTITUDE will determine your ALTITUDE in the business world.

14. ADVERSITY in life is a fact. Your reaction can be to become better or bitter

15. Your management STYLE can be to TERMINATE, DICTATE OR be a GROWTH COACH.

16. Some people will be open minded, some closed minded, while some don't care. Their actions speak louder than their words.

17. Others will remember you for your ability to inspire rather than your ability to discourage them.

18. Some people want to grow personally and professionally while others could care less. That is a fact of life.

19. Cultivate MENTORS in your life rather than tormentors.

20. You can learn from your experiences but a wise person learns from experiences of others.

Study one of these each day to cultivate and accelerate your path to SUCCESS. Inquire about my PEOPLEOLOGY skills workshops to learn many more!

EPILOGUE

Nothing is ever as easy as it seems OR as difficult as it seems. However, understanding these "principles" of SUCCESS is rewarding and worth you effort to master each one. There may only be TWO C'S in the word SUCCESS but learn the NINE C'S that are the real principles.

Keep this book as your study guide. Concentrate your thinking time on one principle at a time for a full month. Make notes to yourself of how you can utilize each and continually improve yourself. Ask for feedback of any blind spots you may have from your mentors, your loved ones and anyone who cares or might benefit from you efforts.

The only difference in the person you are today and the person you can become five years from today are the people you meet and the books you read. Become a student of personal and professional growth with the objective to earn a Phd in helping others to reach their potential with a attitude of gratitude! Only then can we know true SUCCESS.